Hidden Inside

Hidden Inside

Kim Taylor

Delacorte Press

Published by Delacorte Press
Bantam Doubleday Dell Publishing Group, Inc.
666 Fifth Avenue, New York, New York 10103
This work was first published in Great Britain
in 1990 by Belitha Press Limited.

Manufactured in Great Britain
September 1990
10 9 8 7 6 5 4 3 2 1

Library of Congress Cataloguing-in-Publication
Data will be printed in subsequent editions.
ISBN 0-385-30182-0
ISBN 0-385-30183-9 (lib. bdg.)

VERY ORDINARY THINGS, LIKE AN OLD DEAD LOG, sometimes have interesting animals hidden in them. Imagine a hollow tree; inside it there may be a nest, and inside the nest an egg, and in the egg a baby bird. Other animals besides birds build nests. Often they use dry leaves or grass to make a warm bed inside the nest.

The little hedgehogs (*opposite*) were born in a leafy nest hidden under a hedge. Their spines are milky white and very soft. A dormouse (*above*) builds a snug nest inside a hollow tree. Here, the fat little dormouse sleeps soundly all through the winter until it is wakened by the warmth of spring.

Pop goes a pupa

WHEN YOU ARE WORKING IN THE GARDEN, YOU MAY dig up a dark brown sausage-shaped thing that wriggles a little. This is the pupa of a moth. The best way to find out what sort of moth is hidden inside is to leave it on damp earth until it hatches. It may take weeks, but, during this time, a lot that you cannot see is going on inside the pupa.

The pupa started life as an egg, which hatched into a caterpillar, which grew until one day it buried itself in the

4

ground and turned into a pupa. Inside the pupa, all the parts of the caterpillar become mixed up in a sort of white soup, out of which all the parts of a new moth gradually form. The pupa then pops and the moth struggles out. Its body is fat and its wings are crumpled. It pumps a pink liquid from its body into its wings until they are stiff and ready to flap. Before it flies off, it squirts out a few leftover drops of the pink liquid—and away it goes into the air!

Does a cuckoo spit?

*A*BOUT THE TIME THE FIRST CUCKOO IS HEARD IN SPRING, blobs of white froth, like spit, appear on many plants. Country people used to think that the "spit" was left behind by the cuckoo—and so they called it cuckoo spit. But if you look inside a blob of cuckoo spit—like this one on a buttercup stem—you will find that the animal that spat is not a bird at all, but a young froghopper. Froghoppers are insects that suck the juice out of plants. The young froghoppers eat some of the plant juice and blow bubbles with the rest of it. Then they hide inside the mound of sticky bubbles so that birds cannot find them.

Inside a raindrop

IT'S HARD TO IMAGINE THAT ANYTHING COULD BE HIDDEN inside a raindrop. Rain is just clear water, so what can hide in it? Next time it rains, take a close look at a drop hanging from a twig. You will see a tiny picture of the scene beyond the drop. It is not an ordinary picture, because the sky is at the bottom and the ground is at the top! It is an upside-down picture. Each little drop (*above*) has in it a tiny picture of the nasturtium flower beyond. Inside the drop on the rose thorn (*opposite*) is a head-up picture of a tree cricket and beyond, you can see the cricket itself—head down.

Who rolls a leaf?

SEVERAL KINDS OF INSECTS MAKE HOMES FOR THEMselves by rolling up leaves. Leaf-roller weevils make a home for their grubs and a food supply as well. In the picture (*below left*) two oak-roller weevils are getting ready to roll a leaf. They have cut through the leaf on both sides of the mid-rib, and one of them is working on the hanging piece to soften it. The female weevil then lays an egg on the tip of the leaf and starts to roll the leaf upward (*below right*). It is hard work and takes the weevils more than an hour. When the leaf is tightly rolled, the weevils go off to roll another leaf.

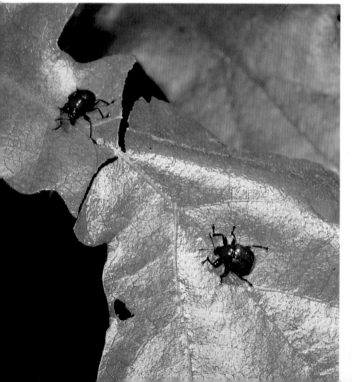

As time passes, the leaf roll turns brown while the rest of the leaf is still green (*below left*). Meanwhile, the egg hatches and the little grub starts to eat the leaf roll from the inside. If you slice through a leaf roll at this stage, you can see the grub in the middle (*below right*). You can also see how cleverly the leaf has been folded to make the roll. When the grub has eaten nearly all the inside of the roll, it turns into a pupa that waits until the next spring before changing into a weevil.

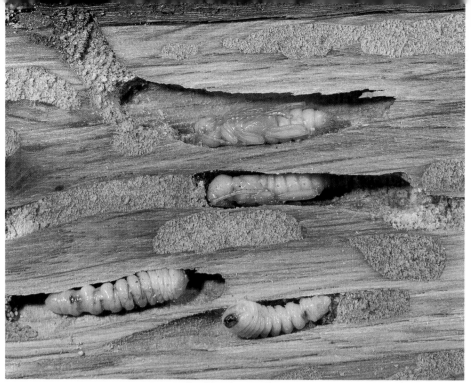

A living log

*I*NSIDE AN ORDINARY-LOOKING DEAD BRANCH THERE MAY be a whole lot of insects munching away. These larvae of a wood-boring beetle have very strong jaws and can chew their way along the branch. Vibrations in the wood warn them when they are near another tunnel and they steer away. When the larvae reach full size, they turn into pupae and rest peacefully at the ends of their tunnels. The beetles have to dig their way out through all the sawdust left by the larvae before they emerge. If you find a dead branch containing beetle larvae, listen carefully —you may hear them chewing away inside!

Babies inside

IN SOME SEASHORE ROCK POOLS THERE ARE LITTLE shrimps that hang in the water close to seaweed. They can be green or brown or transparent. They are called opossum shrimps. Female opossum shrimps have special pouches on their undersides in which to keep their eggs. You can just see the orange-colored eggs in the pouch of the shrimp in the picture. The female keeps the eggs safely in her pouch until they hatch. Eggs in a pouch are much less likely to get eaten than eggs left lying around the pool.

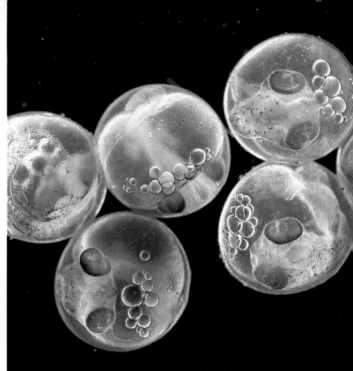

Inside an egg

*A*CLUTCH OF SHIELD BUG EGGS IS HATCHING (*ABOVE left*). Each egg has a lid that opens to let the baby bug out. Some of the eggs have not yet hatched and the eyes of the little bugs show red through the eggshell. Stickleback eggs (*above right*) are nearly transparent and so you can see the little fishes growing inside. Their eyes are big and dark. The bubbles are globules of oil that the little fishes use up as they grow.

The chick inside this hen's egg (*opposite*) is almost ready to hatch. It is packed tightly inside the eggshell. When it starts to hatch, it has to break the egg open with an egg tooth on the tip of its beak.

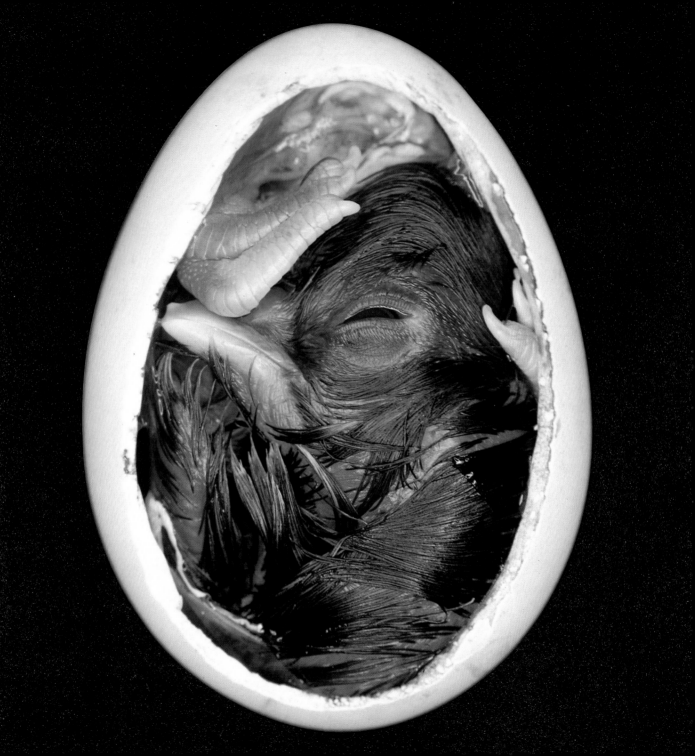

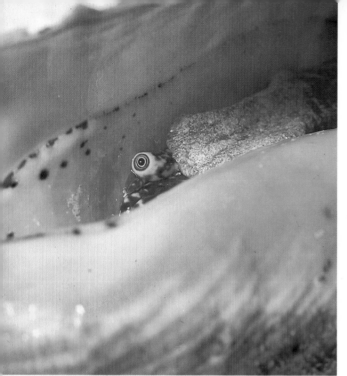

Inside a shell

*A*CONCH IS A BIG, HEAVY SHELL THAT YOU CAN FIND washed up on beaches in warm countries. People sometimes cut the top off a conch shell and blow it like a trumpet. A living conch has a big snail inside with eyes on stalks. An eye is peeping out of the shell (*above left*). When the conch sees that there is no danger near, it puts its foot out of the shell (*above right*) and quickly flips the shell over so that the entrance is facing downward.

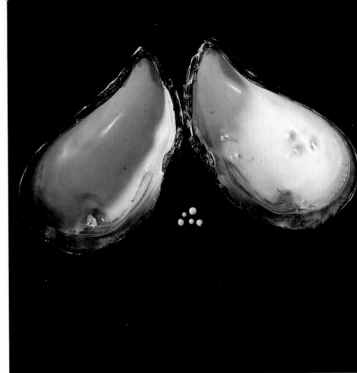

The shell of a mussel is in two halves and normally only opens a crack to let water in. Mussels don't move around, but fix themselves to rocks with threads. If you open a mussel, you may be in for a surprise! As well as the mussel itself, you could find a pea crab (*above left*). How did the crab get in? When it was a tiny larva, it came in through the crack in the mussel's shell and grew to a full-sized crab within the safety of the shell. Sand grains sometimes get in as well and the mussel covers them with hard shell to make tiny pearls (*above right*).

Inside a termite hill

TERMITES BUILD HUGE HILLS OUT OF EARTH THAT bakes hard in the hot sun. A termite hill may contain thousands of termites, but you don't often see them because they stay inside the hill. If you break open a termite hill, you will see hundreds of crawling insects. Some may also have wings. They fly around in clouds when it rains. Some termite hills have a tall chimney that lets out air from tunnels inside the hill. Fresh air can then come in at the bottom of the hill so that the termites can breathe.

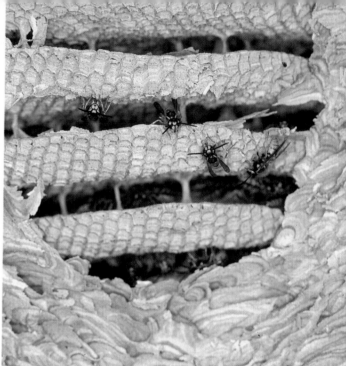

Paper nests

WASPS BUILD NESTS UNDERGROUND, IN TREES, OR EVEN under the roofs of houses. Their nests are made of "wasp paper." With their jaws, they scrape wood from dead trees or fence posts, chew it into pulp, and then pinch it into thin layers of gray paper (*above left*). Inside a wasps' nest are several layers of cells (*above right*). In each cell, a wasp grub lives, hanging head down. Wasps don't collect honey like bees but feed their grubs on chewed-up insects. You can see wasps walking over the sealed cells containing pupae (*opposite*). Some of the pupae have already hatched into wasps.

Inside a stone

SOME ROCKS HAVE CRYSTALS INSIDE THEM, AND OTHERS contain fossils. When you split a rock and find a fossil, you can be sure that you are the first person ever to see that fossil. It has been hidden inside the rock for millions of years until bang went your hammer. The person who found the fossil fly (*above right*) must have been very excited.

The fossil ammonite (*above left*) was found in soft mudstone. While the animal was alive, it lived in the wide part of the shell. When the animal died, this part filled up with mud. The narrow coils of the shell contained air and these gradually became filled with yellow crystals of calcite as the shell became a fossil.

Mudstone sometimes forms hard nodules like giant potatoes. If you break one open, there may be crystals inside. The nodule (*below left*) has been cut in half to show the crystals of calcite that have grown in the cracks inside it. Pudding stone looks a bit like concrete, with rounded pebbles (*below right*) inside. These were washed back and forth and smoothed on a beach many millions of years ago. They then became mixed with mud and sand, which was pressed into stone by the thousands of tons of rock on top of it.

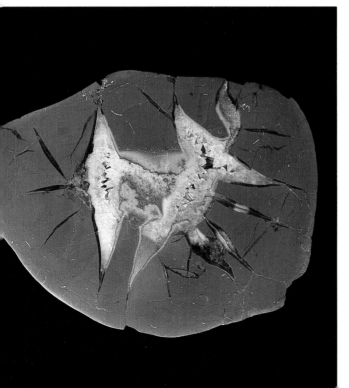

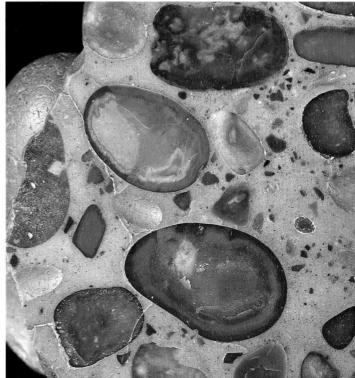

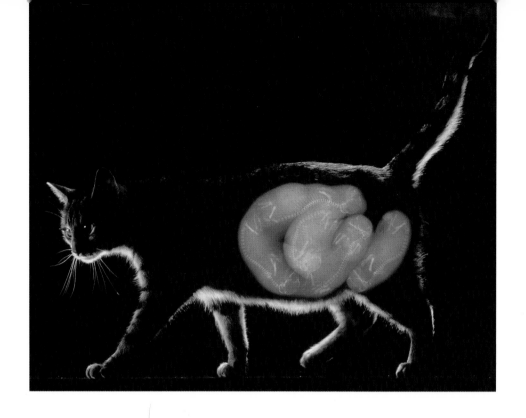

When you see a fat cat it may be just greedy, or it could have babies inside. One way to find out is to shine X rays through the cat. X rays are like light except that they pass through bodies. But they cannot pass through bone so easily and so bones show up in an X-ray picture. Inside this cat, you can see the bones of several kittens. In fact, you can even count the kittens! Each has a skull, backbone, ribs, and legs tucked up under its body. The kittens are nearly ready to be born.

Index